Wonders

Poems about Love and Relationships

Cheryl Batavia

BOOKSIDE Press

Copyright © 2022 by Cheryl Batavia

ISBN: 978-1-990695-50-6 (Paperback)
           978-1-990695-51-3 (E-book)

All rights reserved. No part of this publication may be reproduced, distributed, or transmitted in any form or by any means, including photocopying, recording, or other electronic or mechanical methods, without the prior written permission of the publisher, except in the case brief quotations embodied in critical reviews and other noncommercial uses permitted by copyright law.

The views expressed in this book are solely those of the author and do not necessarily reflect the views of the publisher, and the publisher hereby disclaims any responsibility for them.

BookSide Press
877-741-8091
www.booksidepress.com
orders@booksidepress.com

Table of Contents

Preface i

Youthful Adventures 1
   Boys   1
   Peckerwood's Wedding   4
   Manhood   5
   Flying   5
   Firebird   6
   Rising from the Ashes   6

Adventurous Young Man from Virginia 7
   Connoisseur   7
   Green Apples & Buttermilk   7

Light of My Life 10
   Fellow from Yonkers   10
   Hard Work   10
   Captive Audience   11
   Happy New Year   11
   Mail Order Junkie   12
   Wedding   13
   Bedlam on the Beach   14
   Legacy   14

Lover **15**
    Young Man from the States   15
    My Lover   15
    Rain on the Roof   16
    I Heard Your Name   16
    Remembering   17
    No Regrets   17

Man of My Dreams **18**
    Missouri Boy   18
    Mirror   18
    Evolved Man   19
    Warm, Strong Hands   20
    Adversity   21
    Whisper   22
    I'm Glad I Met You   22
    Mr. Fixit   23
    Blue Sky, Blue Water   24
    Fortune Cookie Moon   24
    Sweet Nothings   25
    Hometown   25
    Wonders   26

*In honor of Robert Louis Snyder, the
Man of My Dreams.*

*My thanks to the Designer, Nadine
Geonson, for making this book beautiful.*

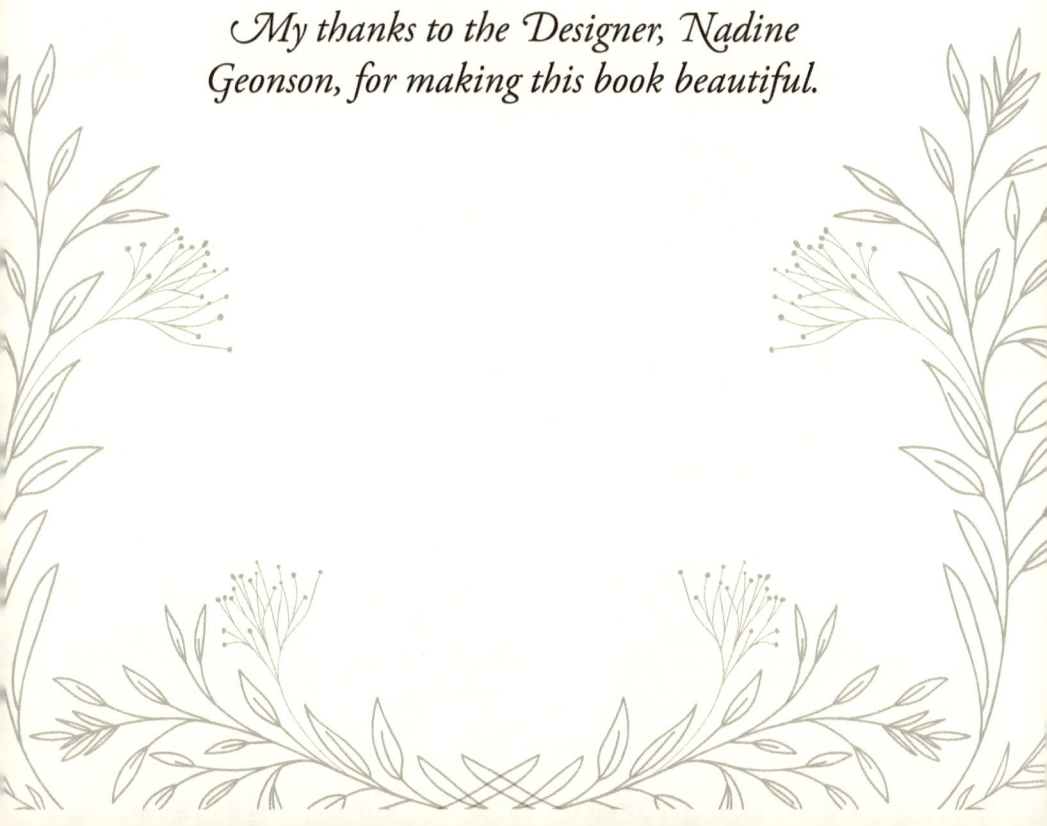

Preface

Men have always fascinated and inspired me. I am sure there are some real jerks out there. I've heard stories about them from credible sources and seen a few in action, but, fortunately for me, all the men I've loved have been wonderful human beings. So why didn't the relationships last forever?

When I was young, boys came and went—nothing serious. Often, circumstances changed or were beyond our control.

As I grew older, there were more fundamental reasons why relationships ended. In some cases, we simply didn't have enough in common, even though there was affection and respect.

I was driven by a desire for connection and often couldn't find the depth of connection I was looking for.

Having friends and brothers is nice, but I didn't want to spend my whole life in that type of relationship. I guess I have pretty high expectations.

The week of my eighteenth birthday, I married a very nice young man, and we had a wonderful daughter together. After eighteen years, we parted amicably, wanting to go in different directions. Our life together is described in the poem, "Green Apples and Buttermilk."

Poems in the "Light of My Life" chapter are inspired by my second husband. For eighteen wonderful years, we shared many adventures and helped each other achieve our mutual and individual goals in life.

I met my second husband when I answered a want ad for a live-in personal assistant for a quadriplegic attorney. Despite breaking his neck in a car accident at age sixteen, he graduated from Harvard Law School and Stanford Medical School.

As a White House Fellow, he drafted regulations for the Americans with Disabilities Act. He worked in the Federal Government, did research, and taught health law at Florida International University. When he died at age forty-five, he left behind a massive body of work. He advocated for the civil rights of disabled people, worked for national health care, and presented amicus briefs in the U.S. and Florida Supreme Courts in favor of assisted dying.

To learn more about his remarkable life and career, read his memoirs, *Wisdom from a Chair: Thirty Years of Quadriplegia*.

My husband was a devoted and very involved father to the brother and sister we adopted from Russia. Sadly, he died seven years after we adopted them.

For the next twelve years after his death, I focused on my teaching career and on raising my children, not dating anyone. Sometimes I was lonely, but I wasn't ready for another relationship. It seemed that whenever I tried to socialize, all I could find to talk about was my late husband.

After my children left home, I began dating online. I communicated with many men and went on a few first dates, but nothing was quite right.

The "Lover" chapter is about a fascinating man I met online. The son of a mathematics professor, he dropped out of school at an early age and worked at a variety of interesting jobs.

At seventeen, he joined the Marines and became a highly decorated war hero, wounded four times in Vietnam. The Marines sent him to college, and he graduated in only three years, despite never attending high school.

He went on to make his fortune in the stock market. He told me, at the age of sixty-nine, that he had retired three times, and might retire again sometime. We enjoyed our time together, but found that we didn't have enough in common to sustain a long-term relationship.

At age sixty-five, I met the man I want to spend the rest of my life with. I sold my house and moved in with him nearly a decade ago. After so many lonely and difficult years, I have never been happier.

The poems in "Man of my Dreams" are a tribute to my significant other. Because of his Southeast Missouri drawl, people may risk underestimating him. If playing Poker with him, that could be a mistake. He is also a formidable Scrabble opponent.

A retired medical technologist, he has encyclopedic knowledge of many subjects, including science, history, politics, and financial markets. He is also good at household repairs, as mentioned in the poem, "Mr. Fixit."

The poem "Peckerwood's Wedding," in the "Youthful Adventures" chapter is about my experiences growing up as the daughter of a Methodist minister in the Blue Ridge Mountains of Virginia.

When country people discovered that my father performed weddings free of charge, many couples came to our house to be married. My mother and I baked them cakes and cut flowers from our garden, and I played wedding music on the piano (badly, I'm sure.)

Sometimes the brides were as young as twelve or thirteen. "Shotgun weddings" were more than a joke. It was an interesting experience growing up in the mountains and meeting those young couples.

Poems in this collection were inspired by the four men in my life I have described, except for the poems in the first section, "Youthful Adventures," which are about various others or are generic.

I hope men will read my poems for a glimpse into a woman's perspective on relationships, and that both men and women will relate to the poems. I think you will find something familiar that makes you say, "Yes, I've been there!"

Thank you for sharing my journey with me. I hope you are enjoying your own journey, and that you are finding happiness and fulfillment in your relationships.

Cheryl Batavia

Youthful Adventures

Boys

When I was seven,
I threw a note under a boy's desk
that said, "I like you."

When I was ten,
I walked with a boy to the Twin Kiss
for an ice cream cone and
sat with him on the porch swing.

When I was eleven,
I roamed barefoot with a boy,
collecting trilobite fossils
and playing "chicken"
with a knife thrown in the ground.

When I was twelve,
I snuggled with a boy
in the back of his grandfather's car
on the way home from church.
When he visited my brother at our house,
we ate taffy from both ends
until our mouths met in the middle.

When I was thirteen,
a boy at summer camp
wrote on the back of his picture,
"Yours Forever."
He wrote me love letters all year
about his football career,
marriage, and raising our children.

At summer camp the next year,
he asked me to return the picture,
so he could give it to another girl!
That was okay;
I spent that summer kissing
another boy across the fountain.

When I was fourteen,
I sang on the church steps with a boy
who played folk songs on his guitar.
We were just friends because,
unfortunately, he thought I was a child.
Later, we wrote friendly letters
while he was stationed in Vietnam.

When I was fifteen,
a boy helped me practice driving
skills in his mother's white Mustang.
While out parking in his father's
baby blue Ford convertible,
we got stuck in a snowdrift.

You guessed it—
my parents were not happy!
When I was sixteen,
I dated a few boys once,
wrote gloomy poems, and
tried in vain to attract the attention
of the "brainiac" of the junior class.

When I was seventeen,
I walked with a boy in the rain
and kissed him under an oak tree.
He was surprised to hear that
I was not interested in love—
just experiences.

When I turned eighteen,
I swore off boys,
married a nice young man,
and grew up.

Peckerwood's Wedding

"Son," Mama said,
"just keep wearin' your pants!"
Peckerwood perked
up at every single dance.
"Don't fool around,"
Pappy told his son,
"or you're gonna be a Daddy
before you're twenty-one!"
Pecker-wood perked up
whenever Sweetie passed.
Her cute little walk
made his heart beat fast!
"Son," Mama warned him,
"There's no harm in lookin'!"
"but before you kiss her,
you better taste her cookin'."
Peckerwood perked up,
no cake or pie in sight,
climbed in Sweetie's window
in the middle of the night.

"Sweetie and her Pappy
are here to see you, son.
Peckerwood was starin'
down the barrel of a gun!

Manhood

Kaleidoscope of genetic possibility,
infinitesimal fraction realized
as human beings.
Monument to procreation,
rising to every occasion,
fulfilling his destiny in quest of pleasure.
Source of comfort and connection,
Muse of architects and poets,
Bringer of ecstasies and anguish,
Builder of dynasties, inciting mayhem,
Worshipped and condemned,
Eternally innocent.

Flying

Uppermost, Outermost,
Bluest Stratosphere.
The air is rare.
We hold our breaths
and do not drift
to outer space,
but, like a feather,
touch the earth.

Firebird

I speak of time...
not of eons, but of instants,
when you burned me.

I was consumed, renewed
by the heat of your body
and the fire of your mind.

Rising from the Ashes

Consumed by the heat of your body,
like the Firebird,
I rise from the ashes.

Seduced by the powers of your mind,
I recreate myself
and fly away with you.

Adventurous Young Man from Virginia

Connoisseur

An adventurous young man
scaled the heights,
eager to see all the sights.
He listened, smelled,
touched, and tasted—
not a moment was wasted
as he experienced
a wide world of delights.

Green Apples & Buttermilk

Green apples and buttermilk.
Swimming at night in the Shenandoah:
the hanging bridge, the knotted rope
in a sycamore tree above the river.
Climbing the tower at seven bends.

Omelets after plays in Middletown.
Yellow roses on my birthday,
White roses on our wedding day.
That's how our eighteen years began.

Our daughter. Her cat named Sunshine
leaving chipmunks on the doorstep
of the house we built above the river.
Chopping wood, baking bread.
Birds outside our window
eating birdseed from our snowy porch.
Homemade soup heating on the grill
as we sledded on the mountain.
Tubing and fishing in the Shenandoah.

Hikes to waterfalls, our daughter
swimming in the icy pools below.
Your beautiful photographs
of Shenandoah National Park.
Ferns and flowers, friendly deer.
Steaks sizzling over oak coals.

The Appalachian Trail,
a Dutch-doored cabin with noisy mice
overlooking farms and towns,
lilacs blooming in the yard.
Climbing the steep trail out of
Nicholson Hollow under a
sky full of stars.

Hiding Easter baskets
for our daughter to find.
Wild turkey and cranberry salad
on the Thanksgiving table
at your parents' house.
Christmas morning breakfasts
of country ham and oyster stew.

The beard you grew for the
bicentennial, helping you cut it off.
You falling asleep
as I painted your portrait.
Your thoughtfulness and tact.
Reaching out to touch you in my sleep.

Handing our new daughter to you
for the first time,
first day of kindergarten,
high school graduation,
rainbow wedding.
Her lifetime of caring and helping others.
She turned out fine, our best joint effort!

These and many other great memories
we made together a very long time ago.
I wish you health and happiness.
You will always be family to me.

Light of My Life

Fellow from Yonkers

A bright young fellow from Yonkers
always drove women bonkers.
Was it the twinkle in his eye
that made women sigh?
That charismatic young fellow
from Yonkers!

Hard Work

I wished you health and success,
so I worked hard.
I wanted you to be proud of me,
so I worked hard.
I wanted you to enjoy life,
so I played hard.
I worked hard because
you worked hard, and
hard work brought a better life
to me.

Captive Audience

Cab Drivers, fellow passengers
on the train,
unwitting victims
in the student lounge,
family, friends, and neighbors—
I told them all
what a great human being you are.

Happy New Year

Happy New Year!
Unlike earlier years,
no resolutions needed—
two years in succession.
We were dreaming big dreams,
supporting each other,
pursuing our goals.

Since that time, life has never
been so perfect that I didn't need
New Year's resolutions,
but it continues to be beautiful
because I dreamed big dreams with you.

Mail Order Junkie

A lapse of your fine, analytical mind,
an insidious malady, compelled you
to buy unique mail order merchandise:
a very reasonably priced knock-off
of Princess Di's engagement ring,
(It's the thought that counts.)
a portable postal scale, toe cushions,
china, monogrammed glassware, a shofar,
and a plaster menorah from Israel.
(I liked the dishes and the menorah.)
In time, you enjoyed a brief remission
of your mail order habit... until the advent
of Ebay, when you relapsed,
and began collecting authentic
Teddy Roosevelt memorabilia—
A noticeable upgrade in taste
from your earlier addiction.
Life with you was a constant delight—
with or without your sad compulsion!

Wedding

Sunny, breezy June day,
children blowing bubbles,
friends and family eating barbecue,
taking photos, dancing to a jazz band.
A chocolate wedding cake
baked by friends.
I never knew a wedding
could mean so much to me,
a celebration of what
has always been true for us:
$1+1>2$.

Bedlam on the Beach

In holiday letters,
you told the story of our family
and life at our house,
Bedlam on the Beach—
a story of love and work and struggle,
energetic children, a devoted dog,
and Thanksgiving dinners
with family and friends.
Thank you for our life together
and for the holiday letter memories.

Legacy

A world of shared experience.
Mountains of pride. An ocean of love.
A legacy of memories. As you always
told me, I'm glad I married you!

Lover

Young Man from the States

A clever young man from the States
always delighted his dates.
His candy was fancy, his jokes were funny,
he danced just like the Energizer Bunny,
and ladies like all of those traits.

My Lover

My lover defines masculinity,
Exceeds expectations
of discipline and honor.
Surpasses standards
of authenticity and truth.
Outshines ideals
of confidence and strength.
My lover smiles his way through life,
knowing, being, loving...
effortlessly iconic.
My lover defines masculinity.

Rain on the Roof

Dawn, rain on the roof,
Magnificent thunderstorm.
Cuddling with you.

I Heard Your Name

I walked through surf,
heart pounding,
blood rushing,
and I thought of you.

The sun warmed me,
cheered me,
and sparkled on the water,
and I saw your smile.

The sea held me,
rocked me, and
gently stroked my face,
and I felt your touch.

The breeze and
the seabirds and
the little waves spoke to me,
and I heard your name.

Remembering

Because pleasure was exquisite,
pain was exquisite, too.
I miss your touch,
but I don't miss missing you.
Better to coil the passion up
and neglect it for a while,
remembering only
the times you made me smile.

No Regrets

I live my life with no regrets.
No tears for remembered joys.
No regrets for risks taken.
No regrets for loving you;
love makes us human!
No regrets for passion,
for pushing the boundaries
of capacity... we know ourselves.
No regrets!

Man of My Dreams

Missouri Boy

A Missouri Boy who speaks with a drawl
is witty and handsome and tall.
He was quite underrated
by women he dated—
I think life with him is a ball!

Mirror

Never met someone
so much like my inner self.
Never expected to,
Never expect to again.
Not male or female,
Not friend or lover.
One speaks what
the other is thinking.
Parallel lives,
Mirrored philosophy,
Shared window on the world.

Evolved Man

Evolved in thought,
Not easily deluded,
Never self-deluded.
Laser-sharp focus on truth.
Divides the goats of reason
from the sheep of folly.

Evolved in intellect,
educated, informed.
Repository of knowledge—
both factual and conceptual,
both trivial and profound.
Grounded, self-deprecating, wise.

Evolved in human interactions,
Eludes the treachery of villains,
never villainous.
Extends himself in acts of kindness,
expecting nothing in return.
Open, vulnerable, self-assured.

Evolved in his passions,
disciplined, moderate, civilized,
slow to anger.
Only in his libido,
primitive man survives evolution!

Warm, Strong Hands

I like a man with warm, strong hands,
and I like the way my hand fits yours.
I like a man who thinks deep thoughts
who talks abstractions
in the middle of the night
in a soothing, Southern drawl.
I like to ride around with a man
who drives like he is seventeen,
but has the wisdom of a sage.
I like a man who is a truth-teller,
a man with honor in his eyes.
I like a man who makes me laugh,
who is silly and witty and wicked.
I like a man with warm, strong arms,
and I like the way I feel in yours.

Adversity

One is defined by actions in adversity
more surely than by polite behavior
in pleasant circumstances.
I know you for your friendly smile,
for kind and thoughtful gestures,
for gentlemanly conduct every day.
You consider my feelings
and tell the truth with tact.
You endure discomfort, uncomplaining,
and graciously forgive mistakes.
You see when help is needed and give it.
What best defines you
is your willingness to spare me
the grief of burying you…
by promising to bury me.
We may, if the future allows us,
both escape that final adversity
and die together.

Whisper

I heard you whisper in my ear
words I wanted to hear you say,
words I wanted to say to you.
Dumbfounded, I lay beside you
and I loved you,
but I didn't say a word.

The words you whispered in my ear
are shouting and singing in my brain.
When I see you again,
I will whisper in your ear.

I'm Glad I Met You

"I'm glad I met you."
Reassuring words to hear
when we are working
to make our dreams reality.
You are the man of my dreams.
I'm glad I met you, too.

Mr. Fixit

Kill the ants, fix a leak
underneath the kitchen sink.
Fill the tires, trim a tree,
take out trash, "doctor" me.

Glue the crystal vase that broke,
tell another silly joke.
Cook the salmon, smile and wink,
laugh and whisper, talk and think.

Play Scrabble. Understand.
Buy me roses, hold my hand.
Play some music, take a drive.
Make me glad that I'm alive.

Hold me close when I cry.
Always love me till I die.
While fixing everything in the place,
you put a smile across my face.

Remember always that I, too,
like to do nice things for you.

Blue Sky, Blue Water

Thoughts turning homeward,
World streaming by,
Blue sky, blue water.

Soaring in the blue,
Like soaring birds,
My thoughts fly to you.

Over the Skyway,
Head in the clouds,
Blue sky, blue water.

Fortune Cookie Moon

Walk with me beneath
a fortune cookie moon, and
wish on every star.

Sweet Nothings

Sugar sprinkle stars,
dark chocolate skies. We
whisper sweet nothings.

Hometown

Years spent wandering
in search of a hometown,
a place to belong,
to know and be known.
You are the closest
thing to a hometown
I will ever know.
I'm glad you were born!
I'm glad we found each other!

Wonders

Dew, wet and cool beneath bare feet.
Bunny munching technicolor grass.
Black racer crossing—elegance in motion.
Green bee sipping breakfast
from an orange flower.

Mockingbird incessantly repeating
his neighbors' songs.
Clouds assemble, palms flutter,
sky darkens, thunder, lightning, shower.
From every tree, birds singing in the rain.

Incandescent sunset.
Stars twinkling in the pine trees.
Water dripping from the leaves.
Frogs singing love songs in the ditches
as we walk hand in hand.

Grass never grew so green.
Stars never shone so bright.
Nature's music—never sweeter!
Wonders of the universe,
shared with the one I love.

www.ingramcontent.com/pod-product-compliance
Lightning Source LLC
LaVergne TN
LVHW040203080526
838202LV00042B/3302